The Kite Story

Freddy and his Kite
A story about entrepreneurship, creativity, and life

Ris K.

The Kite Story

Freddy and his Kite

Copyright © 2017 by Ris K.

Unique Edu Ltd. All Rights Reserved.

Published in United States of America.

ISBN-13: 978-1545416150

ISBN-10: 154541615X

This is a work of fiction. Names, characters, businesses, places, events, and incidents are either the products of the author's imagination or used in a fictitious manner. Any resemblance to actual persons, living or dead, or actual events is purely coincidental.

CONTENTS

Chapter 1: Learning Kite Flying   p.1

Chapter 2: Losing the Kite   p.7

Chapter 3: Building a Kite   p.17

Chapter 4: Creating Fun Kites   p.37

Chapter 5: Developing Fun Kites   p.49

Chapter 6: Growing Fun Kites   p.61

Chapter 7: Going Beyond Fun Kites   p.71

Dear Readers,

Thank you for choosing to read this book.

It is about entrepreneurship, creativity, and life.

I encourage you to read with an open-mind.

Let your thoughts flow.

And enjoy.

1 LEARNING KITE FLYING

Freddy and his parents were celebrating his tenth birthday.

Father: "Happy birthday, Freddy! We got you a kite."

Freddy: "Awesome! I love it! Thank you so much! Dad, let's go fly it now!"

Mother: "Freddy, I don't think this is a good idea. The weatherman said that it would rain today. Besides, it is not a windy day to fly your kite."

Freddy: "But I really want to fly it. Please can we just try? It might not even rain."

Father: "OK, let's do this. The park is not that far away. We can always hit back home if it starts to rain."

Mother, shaking her head in disagreement: "By the

time you reach there, it will be time to go home. What a waste of time."

Father: "Why are we letting someone or something else dictate the plans in our lives? Yes, we should consider opinions and situations but we should not stop doing what we want to do. If we keep hesitating and waiting, we would indeed be wasting our time. I am sure a little rain will not hurt us. It is about learning to adapt to the situation and using the resources we have at hand."

So, off they went. While walking towards the park, his father explained to Freddy the different parts of the kite and their functions. At the park, he showed him how to set the kite in motion and how to fly and control it. Freddy was extremely excited to try it out and was getting impatient with his father.

Freddy : "Dad, I get it. Come on, let me fly it now."

Father: "Hold on. Let me show you how to reel the kite back and you will get your chance to fly it."

After showing Freddy all the basics of kite flying, his father handed the kite over to Freddy. Freddy tried many times but his kite would not fly up in the sky. Freddy, getting frustrated, complained: "There is no wind, Dad. Just like what Mum said."

Father took over the kite and replied: "Your mother might be right, but it is you who choose to believe what she said."

"If you assume what she said was true, then why are

we out here in the first place? It was because you hoped that the predicted outcome would be untrue. However, you cannot just hope and wish. You are responsible to change it."

"There is always wind. You need to be prepared for it. Listen to your surroundings, see the movement of the trees, and feel the wind. Observe and be aware of yourself and your surroundings. Let nature reveal itself to you and adjust your actions to the conditions."

"When I was showing you how to set your kite in motion, you were impatient and distracted. You were letting your imagination run wild and focusing on the future of your kite flying high up in the sky. You failed to pay attention to your present."

"It is good to aspire and have goals but you cannot just focus solely on your goals and the outcomes. You have to focus on the processes. There are five steps – observing, setting the kite in motion, flying the kite, reeling the kite back, and reflecting on your actions."

"Your lesson actually starts right from the beginning when I was describing you the different functions of the kite. Instead, you were selective in your learning."

"Learning how to fly a kite consists of many steps. All these steps are related to one another. To achieve what you want, it is essential to learn things that you may not want to learn."

"You may find certain steps redundant but you will never know when they might come in handy. You may not comprehend everything now, but in time you will understand. Hence, do not skip any step but enjoy the whole learning process."

"You ought to respect the time and effort spent on teaching you. Let me show you again. This time observe, listen, and ask any questions when you are in doubt."

Freddy nodded and gave his full attention to his father. When it was time for him to try, Freddy excitedly took over the kite. At first, the timing of setting his kite in motion was just too early. Then, it was just too late. Freddy practiced several times. Finally, he got the kite up in the sky. At that moment Freddy was so proud of himself.

An hour later, dark clouds were gathering up in the sky.

Father: "It is going to rain soon. Let's pack up."

Freddy: "But I just got my kite up flying. Don't we get the strongest wind during a storm?"

Father: "Yes but it is too dangerous and risky. We have to pick our battles. There will be better days with stronger winds. Talking about this, we should establish certain rules."

Freddy: "Rules? Oh no..."

Father: "Rules will direct you in the right direction. They are supposed to help you and not restrict you. Let's pack up and we can work together on coming up with a set of rules on our way back home. I want your input and your suggestions. In this way, you will be committed."

Freddy and his father came up with the following simple rules for kite flying:

1. Freddy will only fly his kite after he has finished all his homework and chores.

2. His father/mother/designated adult must be present when Freddy is flying his kite at the park.
3. Freddy must be considerate to other people at the park.

4. At any moment when Freddy feels unsafe, he must stop and talk to his father/mother/designated adult.

For the next few weeks, Freddy learned the techniques of kite flying with his father. Each time, he learned:

- when to reel in the spool and when to release it
- when to run with the kite
- when to stop and observe
- when to change direction, be it against the wind or with the wind
- when to go backwards so as to move forward
- when to do nothing
- when to stop flying to replenish his strength
- how to have fun and enjoy the moment

Freddy realized that every second of kite flying required effort and attention. This would start even before flying the kite.

First, he had to understand the weather, pick a good spot at the park, and observe his surroundings. Then, he would set his kite in motion.

Every flying experience had limitations and rules to conform. One could either play the game or have the courage to break the old rules and set new rules. To break old rules and to set new rules, Freddy learned that he must first gain trust, trust from his parents and trust of his own skills and abilities. It was about being flexible and firm, understanding when to control and when to let go, and being aware of the surroundings while focusing on the kite.

Several weeks later, Freddy had mastered the art of kite flying. He could set it in motion during the first try and was able to control it well. Freddy loved kite flying and set his sights on flying his kite higher and further.

2 LOSING THE KITE

It was another day at the park and Freddy was flying his kite with his father.

Freddy: "Look! It is so far high. You can hardly see it."

Father: "That is awesome. Remember to control it."

Freddy was so happy because that was the highest point that his kite had ever reached. Then, Freddy felt a touch of the wind. He knew that he had to pull the line back. However, hoping that he could get his kite higher, Freddy changed his direction and started running.

Father: "Stop! You cannot outrun the wind."

Freddy: "No Dad, I can do it! I am going to fly my kite higher."

Freddy refused and turned. He tugged the line and it snapped. The line fell on the ground and the sail flew away.

Freddy was shocked. He frantically chased after the sail but it was gone. He burst into tears and ran back home.

For the next few days, Freddy was extremely sad and angry. He could not understand why the very day when he had reached his highest point was the very day he lost his kite. He was mad at himself and at the world.

Freddy: "The very day I reached the peak was the day I lost everything. All my effort is gone. This is silly. I hate myself. I hate my life. I hate the world."

Mother: "This is what happens when you put all your eggs in one basket. You put all your passion, time, and effort in kite flying. When it failed, it destroyed you completely. Being passionate about something does not mean you can be great at it. You were never meant to fly that high. Is OK to hate your life. There are millions out there who are hating their lives too."

Father: "It is perfectly fine to feel angry and sad. I want you to vent all your feelings out now."

Freddy: "All those weeks that I have spent practicing kite flying was so stupid. Just like what mum has said I was never meant to fly that high. I hate my life."

Father: "Now, I want you to think about what you have just said. And I want you to laugh."

Freddy: "What are you saying? I do not get it."

Father: "You spent days crying about your defeat. It is time to stop and laugh at your defeat. I want you to laugh because you know those statements are untrue. Because if you don't, then are you saying that you truly honestly hate your life? That those weeks when we had fun flying your kite was really stupid?"

Freddy: "Well..."

Father: "Indeed, deep in your heart you know those statements were untrue. Yet you spent days repeating those statements. Be careful of what you choose to say. Your words have unforeseen consequences. You could have unknowingly hurt yourself and other people."

"We experience life through our feelings and perceptions. Life is a storage of moments. Realize that a moment is just a moment itself. Thinking about a moment is different from the moment."

"Losing your kite is just losing your kite. It has nothing to do with your thinking. By thinking negatively, you have given up your power and your choice of understanding the moment."

"You kept asking why did this happen to you. Well, why not? What is so special about you that you should not lose your kite? It is true at that moment, you were not meant to fly higher. You need to acknowledge your limitations and know where you belong at this point of time."

"But were you never ever meant to fly higher? Do you know that? Does your mother know that? No one knows that. The world has infinite possibilities and the world is constantly changing. One day, it is possible you may even fly your kite up to outer space."

"You do not always get to know the reasons behind the failures. You just have to move on. Being passionate about something means that you will keep moving forward and eventually you will figure out what you are best at."

"If kite flying is what you want, then why would this defeat stop you from moving forward? Did you really lose all the time and effort that you have put in? It would only be if you let this failure defeat you and stop you from pursuing what you really want."

"It is OK to cry and whine but at some point you have to learn to stop. Do not be like those people who continuously hate their lives. You have to break this miserable cycle."

"As parents, we do care about you. But it only can go so far. You have to care about yourself. The question is how much do you care? And do you care enough to change."

"Changing your thinking is the first step. But you cannot just stop at thinking, you have to change your actions. You need to act on it."

"Know when to stop, retreat, and conserve your energy so that you can push your limitations to create a better position at another point of time. Understand that this is not the end but a beginning to a new you."

Freddy listened and realized that losing his kite was actually part of kite flying. The very first step was to acknowledge the lost of his kite and embrace his incompetency. The next step was to motivate himself to change and improve by analyzing his mistakes and develop a plan to prevent recurring mistakes.

Freddy understood that planning and thinking was just the beginning. It was doing that really mattered. To fully grow and improve, Freddy had to actually work on it and act on it. Hence, he mustered up this courage and apologized to his parents and begged his parents to buy him a new kite.

Freddy: "Mum and Dad, I am very sorry for saying things that I shouldn't have said. I do care about my life and do love and treasure my life. I have learned from my mistakes and would like to be given a second chance. I really love kite flying and hope that you can buy me another kite."

Mother: "Freddy, it is great that you have learned your mistakes but winter is coming and you won't be able to fly your kite. It would be a waste of money. Besides, you have far more important things such as upcoming school examinations."

Father: "I am glad that I didn't buy you a kite after you have lost yours. Timing is crucial. When you learn and when you do matters. What you choose to focus on matters. If you are too busy doing, you have no time to learn or to think."

"Going through sadness, anger, and pain is part of life. One way to value life is by standing up and having that much courage to face your failures and learn from them."

"It takes a lot for one to say sorry but it takes a whole lot more for one to say sorry for the right purpose. I am I am sure you will truly value your second chance."

"However, right now, focus on school and we will get you a brand new kite after the examinations. School is important but kite flying can teach you something different. As for winter, it is the harshest times that will help you to learn. Adaptation, flexibility, and faith."

Soon, the examinations were over and Freddy received his new kite. However, he was not as excited as he was before. He feared losing his kite again and was doubtful of his skills and abilities. Although, Freddy really liked kite flying, he would only fly on good days and choose not to fly too high.

Father: "Come on Freddy, let's go kite flying."

Freddy: "But it snowed. It is slippery and dangerous."

Father: "Think positively. Honestly, what is the worst that can happen? We will be fine. It will be fun."

It was cold and windy outside. When they reached the park, it was pretty empty and there were small piles of snow everywhere.

Freddy: "It is just too cold and too windy."

Father: "Can you do anything about this? Can you change the weather?"

Freddy: "No, we cannot."

Father: "So, we have to change ourselves. You are not dressed warmly. How are you going to focus on flying your kite when half of the time you are feeling cold? Remove anything that would divert your focus. Go put on a warmer coat."

Freddy ran back home, put on his snow coat, and went back to the park.

Father: "The park is pretty empty. We have all this space that we did not have previously. We are going to be creative and have lots of fun."

Freddy: "Dad, the truth is the park is empty because there are piles of snow everywhere and it is difficult to move around."

Father: "You have been pointing out the dangers and the difficulties. It is good to be aware. However, you should see them as opportunities of being creative and adaptive. It is about changing your thinking, strategy, and behavior so as to prevent accidents from happening. Yes, some spots are slippery and dangerous. So, we will find a good spot. These piles of snow are just a great way to challenge yourself. You will learn to maneuver around them."

After they found a good spot, Freddy set his kite in motion and fixed his position.

Father: "Son, you can fly it higher."

Freddy, fearing that he might lose his kite, replied: "No, I am comfortable right where I am right now."

Father: "When people become doubtful, they focus on bad outcomes and refuse to move forward. Yes, understand the risks but also understand the odds of that happening. Most people fear things that are never going to happen and hence they end up with no energy to deal with things that really matter."

"If you decide to bring fear into the picture, fear would always be daunting you. Do not let a momentary emotion control and define you."

"Right now, everything that is not in your control has aligned together to create that prefect condition for you to push beyond your boundaries. Do not deny this opportunity given by the universe."

"Do not let negative emotions take over your rational thinking. It is OK to take a chance and let go momentarily. But learn to regain control so as not lose yourself permanently."

"You have mastered the skills of kite flying. You have practiced and you are well-prepared. You are just waiting for the right time and it is now. You might not have a clear view of the outcome but if you make decisions based on your true values and your best knowledge, the outcome would be nothing that you cannot handle."

"Free yourself. The future is unclear but never stop pushing forward. I am not asking you to leap far. I am asking you to just believe and move a small step forward."

Freddy nodded, took a deep breath and slowly released the line. The kite flew higher and was steadily floating in the sky.

Freddy: " I did it!"

Father: "That is great, son! You are always in control. Know when to slow down and when to move forward. When to go high and when to stay low."

"You can stop and rest but do not ever stop moving.

Even if you are inching, at least you are going forward. At some point, you will realize that you could only fly that high but at least you tried to make it to your highest potential. If kite flying is what you want, then treasure every experience and enjoy it. Remember, always have fun."

At that moment, Freddy realized that fear and doubt had stopped him from enjoying what he really wanted. From then on, he treasured every kite flying moment. Sometimes, he was happy when he could fly his kite higher. Occasionally, he was sad that he could not reach that far. At times, he was just content to be in the same position. Either way, he learned how to enjoy all these moments.

3 BUILDING A KITE

One day, while flying his kite in the park, Freddy was approached by a girl.

Wendy: "What is that that you are flying?"

Freddy: "It is a kite."

Wendy: "Can I try?"

Freddy hesitated but greed to share. He trusted Wendy and taught her the basics. Wendy and Freddy would either fly the kite together or take turns to fly the kite. They coordinated well and had great fun.

Wendy: "Freddy, what if I have my own kite?"

Freddy: "That is a great idea. You should ask your parents to buy you a kite."

Wendy begged her parents to buy her a kite. Sadly, they refused. So, Freddy and Wendy smashed their piggy banks in hopes that they would have enough money. Unfortunately, $6 was not sufficient. Hence, Freddy asked his parents for help

Mother: "There must be a reason as to why Wendy's parents would not buy her a kite. We do not know the reasons and should not meddle with other people's affairs. Besides, why would we give away our hard-earned money to another parents' child? We cannot help her."

Father: "People are random and do not need solid reasons to do anything. Acknowledge their reasons but do not let them affect your motivation."

"Nevertheless, we should be grateful that these people cared about what we do and acknowledged our existences. Be thankful for their opinions. Good or bad, we have the power to improvise it. Remember, the most ruthless people are those who completely ignore our existences and ignore our purpose of achieving something."

"It is great that you have found a friend who loves doing what you do and has the same vision as you. The essence of such a special human connection is rare and should be treasured."

"Indeed, we are not in the position to help, not because we are selfish but because you and Wendy have the inner abilities to figure out a solution. Seek knowledge. Learn to build tools and skills to develop solutions. You need to be hungry. Hungry enough to push forward."

"Before focusing on getting a kite, you have to understand why Wendy wants her very own kite. What is the main purpose? Is it because you weren't sharing your kite with her? Or it is because she dislike your kite? You need to know that to find the correct solution."

"Once you have understood the main purpose, focus your energy not on the problem but on the solution. Do not let the problem itself define your next actions. If you don't view it as a problem, there will not be any limitations."

With that in mind, Freddy thanked his parents and talked to Wendy.

Wendy: "My parents said that it was pointless. It was not something worth playing like baseball or tennis."

Freddy: "People can express their opinions but do not let that affect us. Only you would know if kite flying is truly pointless. I bet you do not feel that way, do you?

Wendy: "No, I really do enjoy kite flying. I do not think it is worthless. But I can set aside some time to pursue baseball and tennis as well.

Freddy: "Ya, it is not like you have to give up one for the other. Why do you want to have your own kite?"

Wendy: "Well, it was great flying your kite together but I feel bad having to share your kite. If I have my own kite, we can fly our kites together and it would be different. I want to create my own experience, my experience with you, and our experience."

Freddy: "That is an interesting perceptive. Well, I am glad that it wasn't because you didn't want to spend time with me. "

Wendy: "No, absolutely not. I think we will have more fun if I have my own kite. So, I was thinking why not build a kite?"

Freddy: "Awesome idea. I don't know how to build one. Let's ask our friends."

Freddy and Wendy asked their friends for help but no one knew how to build a kite. One of his friends suggested to post a message on an online help forum. So, Freddy posted the following message:

Attention Kite Fliers!
We are Freddy and Wendy. We love kite flying.
We are sharing a kite.
Wendy will like to have her very own kite.
Unfortunately, we only have $6 and cannot buy a kite.
We want to build a kite and hope someone can help us.
Please send us any suggestions.

Soon Freddy and Wendy received many different ideas. Some of them were:

1. Go to the toy store and ask the store manager for help. (Unfortunately, the store manager only knew how to sell kites.)

2. Use materials that you can find at home to build it. (It did not work.)

3. Give me your $6 and I will build it for you. (Perhaps this might work.)

4. Exchange your kite for 2 of my old kites. (Freddy could not forgo his kite.)

5. Find ways to get more money so that you can buy a kite. (Possible? But this might take a longer time.)

Freddy: "Let's go with the third option and pay Jason to build a kite."

Wendy: "But I want to build a kite."

Freddy: "Why bother when we can just get one?"

Wendy: "Well...I checked the prices of the materials and it will come up to $15. I am not sure why Jason will do it for only $6."

Freddy: "I am sure he is resourceful."

Wendy: "I think we should learn how to build a kite. Let's post another message. This time targeting kite builders."

Freddy agreed and revised the message.

Attention Kite Builders!
We are Freddy and Wendy. We love kite flying.
We are sharing a kite.
Wendy will like to have her very own kite.
Unfortunately, we only have $6 and cannot buy a kite.
If you have ever built a kite, please help us.
Please send us any suggestions.

Once again, Freddy and Wendy received many replies. These were some of the responses:

1. It would cost you $25. $6 won't do the trick.

2. Give me your $6 and run some errands. Then, I will build you a kite.

3. I will build it for free.

Freddy: "Olivia offered to build it for free."

Wendy: "Isn't that too good to be true? I do not trust her."

Freddy: "I chatted with her. She is just a nice old lady who wants to help. She has built kites before. She does not expect anything in return. Besides, we are not doing anything against the laws or our moral values. As long as we are not taking advantage her, we should be fine."

Wendy unwillingly agreed and contacted Olivia. Weeks went by and it was time for Wendy to collect her kite.

When Wendy saw the kite, she frown and said: "This looks terrible. I told you I wanted sky blue. This is dark blue. And the kite is flimsy. I do not want this."

Olivia, shocked at Wendy's reaction, replied: "Young lady, do not be rude. I did the very best I could."

Wendy: "You did nothing at all. I knew it was too good to be true. This is so ugly even if it is free I do not want it."

Wendy threw the kite on the ground and stomped out. Freddy, taken aback by the outburst, went after her.

Freddy: "Why are you so mad?"

Wendy: "The kite was horrifyingly ugly. It is all your fault. You tricked me into working with Olivia. I did not trust her right from the start."

Freddy: "MY FAULT? You are the one who needed a kite. Not me!"

Wendy: "Yes and we should be building it."

Freddy: "I was just trying to help you. Well, you can build your kite without me!"

After yelling at Wendy, Freddy ran back home crying.

Freddy: "Mum was right. I should not have help her. Wendy is so ungrateful. I do not need a friend like her."

Father: "To help Wendy you have to listen to what she was trying to tell you. To listen is to hear, acknowledge the information, and then take the information into consideration. Right from the start, all Wendy wanted was to build a kite. Her main purpose was to have more fun by flying her own kite with you. Her solution to attain this purpose was to build a kite."

"I looked at your online messages. If you are unclear of your focus, you will not target the right group of people. Hence, you will be overwhelmed with unwanted opportunities. You will be tempted to pursue something that deviates from the main purpose. It is pointless to hop on a good opportunity when it is not what you want. You will just be wasting your time and energy."

"You thought that you were helping. However, Wendy did not see it that way. Unfortunately, instead of being assertive and telling you what she really wanted, she chose to go along with your suggestion. If you let other people control where you are going, then you should not blame them when you end up at the wrong destination."

"We must learn to say no. Saying no gives us the power to choose what we want to give our attention to. When we choose to focus on certain actions and ideas, we are projecting our interests and attention on them."

"Wendy did not trust Olivia. Without trust, it becomes more difficult to communicate well. Without trust, you may not appreciate a person's work or see how you can work together to achieve what you want."

"You failed to listen to Wendy and Wendy failed to express herself firmly. This simple miscommunication ultimately led to this huge fight. There are ups and downs in a relationship. To foster a deep relationship, you have to go through difficulties. It is through healthy and meaningful fights that you will learn about yourself. If you care about Wendy, you cannot just give up this friendship."

"Right now, you owe it to yourself to forgive yourself and Wendy. Forgive yourself and be accountable for your past actions. Forgive Wendy but understand only she can be accountable for her own actions. Do not expect her to make amendments just because you forgive her."

"Apologize and talk to Wendy. If she treasures this friendship, she will learn to forgive herself and forgive you too. If she does not, then have grace and forgive such ignorance and move on."

Freddy nodded in agreement and went to apologize to Wendy. Wendy forgave Freddy and acknowledged that she was in the wrong too. They refocused and revised their online message.

Attention Kite Teachers!
We are Freddy and Wendy. We love kite flying.
We are sharing a kite.
Wendy will like to have her very own kite.
Unfortunately, we can't afford to buy a kite.
We would like to build one.
If you know how to build a kite, please teach us.
Please send us any suggestions.

This time, they received numerous responses from many teachers. Some wanted to be paid while others offered free advice. Freddy and Wendy were swarmed with choices and were not sure who they should learn from. Frustrated, Freddy talked to his parents.

Mother: "Beware of people who give freely. They have ulterior motives. People are selfish and greedy. They are willing to lose as long as they could gain more. With $6 you cannot get much. Money can only go so far."

Father: "First of all do not assume. Do not generalize. It is true that there are some people who would take advantage of you. But not everyone is out to get you."

"Before asking for help, you must first ask yourself - what is the purpose of you learning how to build a kite? Understand the underlying reasons. Do not lie to yourself. Be real and authentic."

"When finding a teacher, share this true purpose. The right teachers will push you towards the right path. Some people are good at heart and some are not. You will never really know. All you can do is to be yourself. Open up and be willingly to trust. Be truly genuine and have a passion for learning."

"Realize that it is not only about what you learn, it is also about how you learn. Personalize your knowledge. Improve your learning process. Translate your knowledge from one subject to another."

"Even if you doubt your abilities or are uncertain of the future, give your attention to every learning opportunity. Allocate your effort and time wisely, and know when to stop and switch to another learning opportunity."

"When learning, seek with clarity. Do not assume a teacher's abilities and motivations. It is perfectly fine to have certain judgments. But support your judgments with substantial information. Verify what was said. Observe the actions behind the words. Understand the reasons behind the actions. Do not expect people to give you all the help and do not expect them to guide you all the way."

Freddy's father then took a piece of paper and wrote the following:

Table of Judgments

Good Good Judgment	Bad Good Judgment
Good Bad Judgment	Bad Bad Judgment

Father: "This will help you to make better decisions and to think of ways to change your course of actions. Good and bad judgments refers to the core underlying purpose. Once you have established that, you will move a step further asking what are possible the good and bad outcomes. Let me illustrate using an example."

For example: Should I take up tennis lessons?

Good Good Judgment	**Bad Good Judgment**
Good Judgment:	Good Judgment:
I want to learn a new skill.	I want to learn a new skill.
Good Good Judgment:	Bad Good Judgment:
I really like tennis and I play well.	I am terrible at tennis and wasted my money on tennis lessons.
Good Bad Judgment	**Bad Bad Judgment**
Bad Judgment:	Bad Judgment:
I want to learn tennis because I want to show off my skills.	I want to learn tennis because I want to show off my skills.
Good Bad Judgment:	Bad Bad Judgment:
I found out that I am good at tennis and I like this sport.	I am terrible at tennis and my schoolmates laughed at me and I wasted my money on tennis lessons.

Father: "Ask yourself if it is a good judgment or a bad judgment? If it is good, then what should you do to prevent bad good judgment from happening and what should you do to achieve good good judgment."

Good <u>Good Judgment</u>	**Bad <u>Good Judgment</u>**
<u>Good Judgment</u>:	<u>Good Judgment</u>:
I want to learn a new skill.	I want to learn a new skill.
Good <u>Good Judgment</u>:	Bad <u>Good Judgment</u>:
I really like tennis and I play well.	I am terrible at tennis and wasted my money on tennis lessons.
Yes, I will learn tennis.	**Yes, I will learn tennis.**
How to achieve:	How to prevent:
- Practice and keep track of my progress - Have good equipment.	- Ask for trial lessons. - Sign up for only a few lessons.

Father: "If it is a good bad judgment, ask yourself what are the odds of that happening? If the odds are high, then go ahead but only if you are willingly to change your purpose."

Good <u>Bad Judgment</u>	**Bad <u>Bad Judgment</u>**
<u>Bad Judgment</u>: I want to learn tennis because I want to showoff my skills. Good <u>Bad Judgment</u>: I found out I am good at tennis and I like this sport. Odds of that happening: 70% How I know? I have played tennis before and I can gauge my skills. **I will learn tennis but I will change my purpose.** New Purpose: I want to take tennis lessons so as to find out if I am really good at this sport. This purpose becomes a good judgment and can be further categorized into Good Good Judgment and Bad Good Judgment.	<u>Bad Judgment</u>: I want to learn tennis because I want to showoff my skills. Bad Bad <u>Judgment</u>: I am terrible at tennis and my schoolmates laughed at me and I wasted my money on tennis lessons. **No, I will not learn tennis.**

Another example: Should I lend money to Steven?

Good Good Judgment	**Bad Good Judgment**
Good Judgment:	Good Judgment:
I want to help Steven. He is a good friend.	I want to help Steven. He is a good friend.
Good Good Judgment:	Bad Good Judgment:
He managed to resolve his financial problems.	He gambled and lost all the money. He became financially worse.
Yes, lend him money.	**Yes, lend him money.**
How to achieve:	How to prevent:
- State clear lending terms.	- Offer to lend him a small sum of money.
- Offer emotion support. Help him with his gambling addiction.	- Ensure that the money is put into good use.

Good Bad Judgment	**Bad Bad Judgment**
<u>Bad Judgment</u>:	<u>Bad Judgment</u>:
I want Steven to owe me a favor.	I want Steven to owe me a favor.
Good <u>Bad Judgment:</u>	<u>Bad Bad Judgment:</u>
He managed to pull through the financial crises.	He gambled and lost all the money. He became financially worse.
Odds of that happening: 20% How I know? This has happened many times and he did not stop gambling.	**No, do not lend him money.**
No, do not lend him money.	

Father: "Once you have made a decision, you must be committed. Your actions must honor your purpose. Now, even if you were foolish to trust the insincere or to commit to a path that you were blindsided to, it is OK as long as you stop and change. You are not back to the starting point because you are actually changing your course. I would rather that you pick a teacher, pick a path, get hurt, failed, and learn to change, than to hesitate, worry, and not move forward."

"With money, you can purchase materials as well as a person's labor and time. A skillful person would require less time and effort. I advise you to find a skillful person that already has the materials, and his/her effort and time is already made possible either by himself/herself or by someone else."

Freddy shared what he learned with Wendy.

Wendy: "Your dad is right. We should stop analyzing whether a teacher is good or not and just start learning. Your mother is right too. We only have $6 and can only do so much. Why don't we learn from everyone that was willingly to teach us for free?"

Freddy: "That's is a good idea. We will do that. We will dip our toes in the water."

For the next few days, Freddy and Wendy learned that:

- People who built great kites might not be the best teachers.
- People who were not into kite flying, for instance physicists and engineers, could offer different insights.
- People rarely shared every single detail. Intertwining details together from different sources might help.
- Opinions and facts were frequently jumbled together. Checking the source of the information might be useful.
- Helpful people might not offer the best or correct solutions. There were no bad advice, just advice that required improvisation. Regardless, it was important to thank everyone's help.

Although Freddy had this pool of information, it still did not help him or Wendy. Freddy felt very frustrated and unhappy.

One day in school, Freddy accidentally bumped into the principal, Mr Walsh.

Mr Walsh: "What is the matter, Freddy?"

Freddy: "I am sorry, Mr Walsh. I have this problem."

Freddy then went on to explain the whole situation.

Mr Walsh: "Freddy, you have gathered so much information yet you are still finding someone to give you the solution. If you keep thinking about the details, you are not doing it. If you keep thinking about building a kite, then you are not building it. Stop asking and realize that you have to be in action and try things out. If you have not touch any material or piece anything together, how could you expect to build a kite?"

"Learning more and gathering more information might not help you. It is not the amount of time spent on accumulating knowledge, it is the quality of knowledge that matters. All the advice you received is useful but some of them may be useless in your current context. You have to remove the clutter to see clearer. Simplify and reduction will help."

"Also, it seems like you are over-analyzing. Stop seeking for that one perfect solution. Solutions are not easy to figure out but they are usually simple. Now, go find Mr Art, the Grade 8 Art teacher. Tell him I send you and he will help you."

And so, Freddy went off to find Mr Art.

Mr Art: "I am not a kite expert. I am not a kite flier, nor a kite builder or a kite teacher. I did built some kites ten years ago. Frankly, I do not remember how to do it but with all the information you got, I believe we can figure it out. Besides, we have all these materials in this art room at our disposal."

Because Mr Art was no kite expert, he was opened to try out many ideas. They created many different types of kites, and constantly accessed, modified, and tested the kites out in the school field.

Freddy learned that designing was part of building. Materials and kite designs affected feasibility, durability, and flexibility. He also discovered that decorating such as painting and drawing was a great way to personalize his very own kites.

Eventually, Mr Art and Freddy figured out the fundamentals of a good kite. Armed with that knowledge, Freddy built a few simple kites.

Freddy: "Mr Art, thank you so much for helping me. Look, I have built some kites. I am going to show them to Wendy and teach her how to build a kite."

Mr Art: "Hold on, the kites that you built are awful. Look at the spines. One is short and the other is long. And the sail of this kite is not sturdy.

Freddy: "But they fly perfectly fine."

Mr Art: "Freddy, when you get ready for school, do you wear your pajamas or change your clothes?"

Freddy: "I will never wear my pajamas to school. I want to look presentable."

Mr Art: "What's wrong with pajamas? Just like what you said. They are clothes and are perfectly fine."

Freddy: "That is a different issue. This is about how I look."

Mr Art: "There is no difference. The kites that you built are a representation of you. You might not be the best-looking person in school but you have certain standards. Similarly, you are not building the best kites, but you ought to have certain standards. How can you teach Wendy or anyone else when your own kites are sloppy?"

Freddy realized that it was not about building a kite, it was about building a kite with certain standards. He also learned to appreciate and took good care of his kites. By doing so, he developed a sense of pride in building, decorating, and flying kites.

Freddy took a few days to fix his kites. Then, he proudly showed them to Wendy and taught her how to build and decorate her very own kite. With their new kites, Freddy and Wendy enjoyed many kite flying adventures together.

4 CREATING FUN KITES

One day, Freddy and Wendy were flying their kites at the park when a lady approached Wendy.

Mrs May: "Your kite is so special. Where did you buy it? I would like to get one for my daughter."

Wendy: "You can never get this from anywhere else. I did not buy it. I made it and decorated it myself."

Mrs May: "That must be fun. Could you buy the materials and teach my daughter, Kathy, how to build and decorate her own kite? I will pay for the materials."

Wendy: "I am not sure where to buy the materials. Freddy was the one that help me. I am sure he will help you too."

Freddy agreed to help. To get the materials, he went to Mr Art who directed him to a local art store. Once he had the materials, he then showed Kathy how to build, decorate, and fly her very own kite. Soon, all three of them started flying their kites together at the park.

A few days later, another parent spotted them and requested Freddy to help his child to build his own personalized kite. Days later, another parent had the same request. Freddy was happy to help but felt that he could actually create something more.

Freddy: "Wendy, I am thinking of setting up a small kite business. The materials at the store cost $10. I am going to charge an extra $5 for providing the materials, helping the children to build and decorate, and teaching them how to fly the kite."

Wendy: "Good thinking! You should do that for all new customers. "

And so, Freddy started a small kite business. As he became overwhelmed with more and more customers, he hired Wendy and Kathy to help. Soon, the park was swarmed with people building, decorating, and flying their own personalized kites.

Mr Smith, a toy manufacturer, spotted this trend and felt that some of the materials could be replaced with something cheaper. Soon, he developed the "Build-A-Kite" kit which consisted of four simple building pieces, decorative stickers, and paint.

Instead of building a kite from scratch, a child would only have to attach the pieces together. A simple online video on how to build, decorate, and fly the kite was also included. Costing just $10, many began to consider Build-A-Kite as a better option of building kites in the comfort of their homes.

Build-A-Kite had an impact on Freddy's business. Freddy knew he had to do something. After discussing with Wendy and Kathy, they came up with several suggestions:

1. Offer something similar to what Mr Smith is offering (Is that what the children want?)

2. Replace the materials with some thing cheaper (Possible? But how?)

3. Cut costs by sharing the decorative materials (Possible? But how?)

4. Expand the business to another park to attract more kite fliers (Possible? But how?)

5. Show that we are better than Build-A-Kite (Possible? But how?)

They did some research, tested some of the ideas, and found out:

- Replacing the materials with something cheaper could compromise the value. This could also be a safety issue. To develop a cheaper and better material would require more time. This would not resolve the current situation quickly but it should be a long-term goal so as to stay competitive in this market.

- Cutting costs had an impact on the perceived value of the kites. Materials must perform the basic functions. Kites must be kites. It was not about getting the best material, it was about developing a strong imagined image of the material. Promoting the sharing of decorative materials ironically resulted in people taking more than what was required as they felt there was a limited supply.

- Expanding the business would require more resources in managing the new environment. A new environment might not guarantee more customers. One should focus on creating value in the current customers, learn from them, and trust them to provide information on when and how to expand the market.

Freddy did not know what to do and shared his frustration with his parents.

Mother: "Build-A-Kite is cheaper than what you are offering. Why would someone pay more to get the same outcome?"

Freddy: "It is not the same. Unlike Build-A-Kite, we offer people the chance to be creative and have fun. We do not sit at home and build kites. We build kites together. We play together. We bond together."

Mother: "Yes, you are right. But do the children know that? Do they even care about bonding? Ultimately, they just want to have a kite and most people will pick the cheapest and the easiest way. It takes effort to learn to build something. That is why they prefer Build-A-Kite. It is simple."

Father: "People who choose Build-A-Kite are losing out on the essence of what you can offer. Similarly, people who choose you are losing out on the essence of what Build-A-Kite can offer. People have different goals and desires. Understand that products are there because they are fulfilling different goals and desires."

"Build-A-Kite is fulfilling the goals of a group of people and you are fulfilling the goals of another group of people. Build-A-Kite is tangible. Some people prefer to see and feel the tangible benefits before fishing out their wallets. What you offer is intangible. Learning, bonding, and having fun are intangible and subjective benefits. To some customers, what you offer might not be better but it is certainly something different. "

"Build-A-Kite can help your business to grow. Accept that Build-A-Kite is a challenger and you are a worthy opponent. You have to seek the right opportunity to change. Do not change because you fear Build-A-Kite. Do not change because you want to be like Build-A-Kite. Do not change because you see this as a problem."

"Change only when it is an opportunity to improve and grow while still adhering to your purpose. Your purpose is to offer people the chance to bond and have fun playing kites."

"Mr Smith has created a very simple, fun, and affordable toy. Before Build-A-Kite, no one realized that building and decorating your very own kite could be so easy and fun. It creates this craze which is a great opportunity for you. You have to ride with it. Promote your offering to as many people as possible so as to attract new customers who are looking to fulfill their desires with what you are offering."

"When challenged, learn to pivot. Learn to see things differently. Must people learn how to build and decorate a kite before learning how to fly a kite? No, they can learn to how to fly a kite and then learn kite building and decorating skills."

"Realize that Build-A-Kite customers can also be your customers. Do people only want to build and decorate a kite? No, they want to fly it. And this is where you come into the picture."

After listening to his parents' advice, Freddy decided to focus on promoting his kite flying skills. To prove that he was better than Mr Smith, he enrolled in professional kite flying classes.

Then, Freddy launched kite flying lessons. He categorized his methods into three different levels and created comprehensive curriculum for each level. He trained Wendy and Kathy to be kite flying teachers whose main focus was to advance students to the next level.

Freddy posted advertisements on kite flying lessons, showcased online teaching videos, and even offered free introductory lessons. However, this did not improve his kite business. Instead, the number of customers decreased. Freddy was puzzled and shared this problem with his parents.

Mother: "If I want my children to master kite flying, I will send them to those classes that you took. Why will I choose you? You are not the best kite flier or the best teacher. You forgot your true purpose of your business and failed to see the whole picture. This is not playing a piano. You do not need lessons after lessons."

Father: "Previously, I advised you to focus on kite flying but I did not ask you to change your business to focus solely on kite flying. By focusing on processes, operations, and products, you have failed to build relationships. Know that people matters and it all starts with people."

"You need to know who exactly should you be focusing on. If you keep thinking about winning, you have forgotten about growing. If you keep thinking about Build-A-Kite's customers, you have neglected yours. It is not about being better than Build-A-Kite, is it about growing your business."

"Figure out your main competencies. You can't just focus on one. There are actually four aspects to focus on – kite building, decorating, flying, and teaching. At this moment, you are not the best kite builder, decorator, flier, or teacher. You are a master of none. And that is OK because all four roles are crucial in your business. It is not about being best at one thing. It is about finding the right balance and synchronizing all these roles to attain something better."

"Every business is actually a platform for teaching something. Your business is to teach kite building, decorating, flying, and teaching. When teaching, you have to know when to guide your students/customers/employees and when not to. Sometimes, you have to stop talking and start observing. Let them open up themselves to you. Understand their strengths and weaknesses. Discover their untapped potentials, and support their personal dreams and purposes."

"The other day, I saw two girls under the tree happily decorating their kites. All they wanted to do was to decorate kites. Did they try to fly their kites? Yes, they did. They tried but decided that decorating was more fun. Was this bad? Not at all. Even though the kites were too heavy to fly, the girls were perfectly contented because they knew they wanted to be kite decorators. "

"When a person decorates a kite, is he or she learning something? Yes. When a person flies a kite, is he or she learning something. Yes. Every action is a learning experience. Let your students/customers/employees pick and shape their experiences."

"You cannot teach everything. Have faith in people to figure things out for themselves. You need to make them feel smart and capable. They need to feel that you value their input. It is figuring out that makes it fun and meaningful. You have to excite and inspire your students/customers/employees to keep creating this learning experience. It is a continuous cycle."

"Let your students/customers/employees choose their own paths and create their own goals. Only when a person choose to proceed because of own choice, then he or she would accept the challenges and push beyond boundaries. If they choose to be decorators, then show them the world of kite decorating. Learn with them. Have fun and grow together. Encourage them to inspire and teach other people to become kite decorators."

"You have to guide Wendy and Kathy as well. When you hired them as employees to help your business, you are responsible for guiding them. How you push them to fulfill their potentials will impact how they inspire your students/customers."

"When you decided to have this small kite business, it is no longer about you and your own interests. It is not power over people, it is power to lead and transform. It is about pursuing your interests while fulfilling other people's interests. When you are helping other people to reach their potentials you are also helping yourself to achieve. Leverage your power to help others. If you involve your customers and your employees, they will grow with you personally and with your business."

"Your business has created this environment for kite builders, decorators, fliers, and teachers to come together. Each and every one is different. Yet, all of them have something in common. They are passionate about kites. The clashing of all these different personalities and abilities is the gateway to innovation and creativity."

"Build-A-Kite does not offer this. Neither do those professional kite flying classes. Hence, you are offering something that no one else is offering in this the kite industry. Develop that and be the best in offering that."

Freddy thanked his father for his advice and shared it with Wendy and Kathy.

Wendy: "Even though Build-A-Kite has taken some of our customers, Kathy and I were still very passionate to help these children. When these children build and fly their own kites, the excitement and fun is contiguous. But this has changed when you decided to focus solely on kite flying and to control the outcome of the growth of each child. Growth can be guided but it needs to be spontaneous and genuine. Is like planting a seed. We can pick the location and help by providing water and minerals but it is the seed itself that chooses when and how to grow itself ."

Kathy: "We chose to help your business because we were passionate about kites. Wendy likes kite flying and I like kite decorating. We might like different things but ultimately we love to help people to create their own fun kite experiences. Your business has brought kite lovers together. It is like a community of kite lovers. Just like what your dad said, this is definitely something special that we should treasure and develop."

Freddy also chatted with other customers and learned that:

Richard: "This was a place where I could choose who I want to be. I could be a kite flier one day or a decorator another day. But ever since you launched the kite flying program, you have stunted the growth of my imagination. It seems like you are trying to control who I want to be. Soon, I felt a lack of self-respect and I was no longer having fun."

Tim: "If you keep focusing on kite flying techniques, what about the kite? Is like a photographer that keeps focusing on his skills and has completely forgotten about his camera. The very tool that has a life of its own. I used to have such pride just carrying my kite to the park but I no longer feel that way."

Mabel: "I used to keep coming back because I could build new kites all the time. There were always new people and new ways of building kites. I get to learn from them. My mother used to say this - Life is always changing and we have to be quick to adapt. I evolve and change my kites too. But I have stopped coming back because there there were no new people and no new things to learn."

After listening to all the feedback, Freddy refocused and changed his business into a community named "Fun Kites". Then, he worked with Wendy and Kathy to develop the following:

Fun Kites Mission

Inspire kite lovers to have fun learning and growing together.

Fun Kites Culture

We will respect who we want to be individually: kite builder, decorator, flier.

We will learn together. Everyone will be a teacher.

We will inspire each other to grow together.

We will have fun playing with kites together.

Freddy shared this mission and the culture with the Fun Kites members. He emphasized that Fun Kites would be a fun and respectful learning environment for all kite lovers. He also explained that the adoption of this culture was crucial in aligning personal goals with the Fun Kites' mission.

Fun Kites members would come together every Saturday. There were no membership fees and no purchase was required. People could either bring their own kites or buy materials to build and decorate new kites. People who had Build-A-Kite kites were welcome to fly their kites. Fun Kites became a space where kite lovers could express their ideas and emotions freely. It gave people the chance to embrace learning and growing together. Soon, more and more people flocked to the park to join Fun Kites.

At times, there were some who disrespected other members or refused to learn, teach, or bond together. Freddy would explain to them that kindness and trust were essential to the foundation of this community. Instead of focusing on personal gains or selfish intentions, people should open up and work together to achieve something greater. Even if they doubt their abilities or purposes, they should trust that Fun Kites would guide them to find their true selves as long as they were willingly to put in the effort and passion.

These people were given multiple opportunities to change. Freddy understood the need to be the bigger person and to have the grace to give people second chances. If they refused to change, Freddy would let them go. Not because they were bad people, but because were they meant to flourish in another community. Instead of retaining them and ruining the experiences for other people, Freddy would rather that they leave and move on so as to find where they truly belong.

Eventually, Freddy's kite business became more than just a business. It became a community where kite lovers through building, decorating, flying, and teaching learned to trust, bond, grow, and inspire one another.

5 DEVELOPING FUN KITES

One day, Freddy and his father were having a chat after a Fun Kites gathering.

Father: "I have participated in several Fun Kites gatherings and you have done a good job. However, I feel that the members need some guidance. Like a clear direction. Right now, what you have is a group of people coming together to bond and share ideas freely."

Freddy: "I am not sure what you meant. I have established clear building, decorating, flying, and teaching steps."

Father: "Indeed, but there is something more. I advise you to go back to the beginning. Look at the little details. Understand the underlying nature of every occurrence. Explore beyond your Fun Kites community."

"Be patient and you will discover something special that has always been within your community. You just need to capture and shade light on it."

So, Freddy started from scratch. He built, decorated, and flew his own kites. Then, he participated in many Fun Kites gatherings and listened to all the stories shared among the members. At times, he would reflect his ideas in solitude.

Additionally, Freddy started to explore outside the Fun Kites community. He visited many toy stores, art shops, manufacturing facilities, and science centers. He even took up art, business, and science classes. After exchanging many ideas with people from all walks of life, Freddy would share what he had discovered with the Fun Kites community.

One day, as Freddy was looking at a kite design, it hit him. He realized that every kite was different. Every Fun Kites member was creating an experience. Every experience was different. They were all uniquely personalized. This was possible because every person wanted to have something of their very own. Right from the beginning, they were motivated to be different.

Freddy also discovered that what really mattered was how one would react to the experience - the feelings and thoughts of the experience. If Fun Kites could help to shape the perspectives and point out different possibilities, then Fun Kites could change the members' experiences.

Freddy shared his thoughts with Wendy and Kathy. Together, they developed the F Formula – a framework to think creatively with focus. It would guide people to think differently and push beyond boundaries while understanding their personal purposes and their impact beyond a personal level.

F Formula

```
              ┌─────────────────────────────────────────┐
              │ Further                                 │
              │ Feasible  ----->            ----->      │
    Faith     │                  Flexible          Focus│
              │ Firm      <-----            <-----      │
              │ Fun                                     │
              └─────────────────────────────────────────┘
```

A very simple example is illustrated below to explain the F Formula. Each F is broadly defined. Depending on the context, certain details for each F may not be applicable. One can choose how wide or how narrow one wishes to define for each F.

Faith: With regards to this situation, do I believe in myself? Do I believe in my abilities to deal with this situation? Do I take responsibility for every outcome? Do I trust the people, things, nature, society, and the universe that are affecting my situation? Faith is needed right from the start. Faith encourages people to think positively and have the courage to move forward. (Note: The universe refers to everything - the known and unknown. It consists of infinite possibilities.)

E.g. Before building a kite, I have faith in myself. I believe in my abilities and know that I am able to accomplish this goal. I also have faith in my teacher. I know that my teacher has the knowledge to help me. I am thankful to be given this learning opportunity.

Flexible: How can I ensure further, feasible, firm, fun, and focus are all aligned together? Flexible ties the framework together.

Further: How can I go beyond boundaries? What are some of the distorted, impossible, and exaggerated ideas? What is my ideal concept? How can I think differently? Is this challenging? Does it help me to grow? How sure am I about this?

E.g. What if my kite is like a cloud floating in the sky? So, I am going to use cotton wool to decorate my kite. My teacher said that no one has done this before. This will be challenging. This is a good opportunity to explore something different.

Feasible: What are my limitations? Can this be done? Is this within the budget, resources, time, and commitment? What are the rules? What are my strengths and weaknesses? How sure am I about this?

E.g. The deadline for this project is next month. I have sufficient time. I am committed to this idea but I do not have the money to buy cotton wool. I have good kite flying kites but I am not sure if my kite can fly with cotton wool on it. (Go to "Flexible" to find solutions.)

Solution: I will borrow some cotton wool from my parents. To ensure that my kite flies, I will only use a small amount of cotton wool. I will carry out trial and error. I may need a bigger kite or improvise my kite to ensure better wind flow. I will share my concerns with my my teacher.

Firm: How do I achieve stability? Can this withstand? Is it reliable? Is it durable? Can I trust this? How sure am I about this?

E.g. I have to make sure that the cotton wool will stick on my kite. How do I attach the cotton wool on my kite? Super glue, perhaps? How do I ensure that the cotton wool will remain attached on my kite? Tape? Sewing it? What are some other uncommon methods? Will this be within my budget and how do I make this work? (Go to "Flexible" to find solutions).

Solution: I will research on these methods and find other suitable methods. I will conduct tests and keep track of my budget.

Fun: Do I enjoy this? Do I like what I am doing? Is this fun? Is it likable? Is it attractive? How sure am I about this?

E.g. Yes, this will be fun and enjoyable. I am happy with this idea.

Focus: How mindful and aware am I? Focus has four aspects. It is broadly defined below.

Inner self: How does this affect me? Why am I doing this? Is this what I want? Does this align with my purpose? Does this achieve my short-term and long-term goals? What are my gut feelings?

E.g. I choose to do this because this is me. This is my style. This is what I want. I feel great. It achieves my short-term goal of being a kite decorator and aligns with my long-term goal of being a fashion designer.

Inner circle: How does this affect the people around me (people inside my social circle e.g. family, friends, classmates, teammates, etc.)? What do they think about this? What are their opinions and emotions?

E.g. My friends thought that it was a great idea. But my parents felt that I could do something more creative (Go to "Flexible" to find solutions).

Solution: I will still use cotton wool because this is what I want. To be more creative, I will create different shapes and designs. I am aware that this will affect feasibility and stability.

Outer circle: How does this affect other people (people outside of my social circle e.g. Fun Kites, school, society)? Is this for the greater good? What do they think about this? What are their opinions and emotions?

E.g. Many Fun Kites members considered this as a new idea and welcomed it. I am helping other members to grow creatively by expanding the pool of knowledge.

External circle: Is this morally right? Where does this stand in my life? Is this what I am meant to do in this world?

E.g. Cotton wool does not pollute the environment. I am not stealing another person's idea. This is helping me to develop designing skills. I do see that I am meant to be a designer some day.

After using the F Formula, the next steps would be to organize clear and simple action plans. In this case, some some action plans could be stating clear goals and deadlines for this decorating project, and listing specific steps for trial and error. One would then proceed to carry out the project and revisit the F Formula to ensure that the actions are in alignment.

Freddy introduced the F Formula to the Fun Kites community. This formula would shape thoughts and actions; and assist with learning and teaching within the community. To guide the members on using the F formula, Freddy decided to train a pool of leaders by launching the "Fun Kites Leadership" program.

These leaders had the following qualities:

1. A passion for kites (I like what I do.)

2. Believe in Fun Kites (I trust this community to take care of me. I belong here.)

3. Moderate or high level of kite building, decorating, and flying skills (I have the essential knowledge.)

4. Help other members to grow (I have a desire to help members to grow in the positive direction. I am sensible, kind, understanding, and patient. I communicate well. I know when and how to guide and when not to.)

5. Strive to continuously learn and improve (I am curious. I challenge the norms and constantly seek new knowledge to improve myself and the Fun Kites community.)

6. Care beyond Fun Kites (I care about my members' personal life purposes and goals. Together, we shall create something meaningful and impact beyond the community.)

Each leader would guide each individual on fully utilizing the F Formula when acquiring kite building, decorating, and flying skills. The leader would supervise and give clear and simple directions, and motivate and challenge the individual to think differently. After acquiring the basics, the individual would then explore beyond Fun Kites.

Then, leaders and individuals would to come together to share new and old ideas and to think as a team. Through this, individuals would get the opportunity to switch roles and teach and inspire one another. Subsequently, different teams would come together to create more diverse teams.

Fun Kites members were encouraged to consider Fun Kites as a safe place to open up and share their personal goals and life challenges. Using the F Formula, members would help one another to achieve personal goals as well as Fun Kites goals.

Step 1: Learning

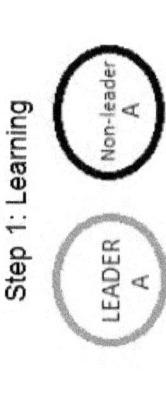

- Leader supervises and guides. Teaches kite building, decorating and flying skills.
- Individual learns about Fun Kites mission and culture. Use F Formula to think differently.
- Figures out strengths and weaknesses, self-purpose and personal goals.

Step 2: Exploring

- Individual is encouraged to explore and gain knowledge outside of Fun Kites.
- Share any new knowledge with the leader and gain feedback. Leader gains new insights
- Shapes personal goals and purpose. Align them with Fun Kite's mission.

Step 3: Sharing

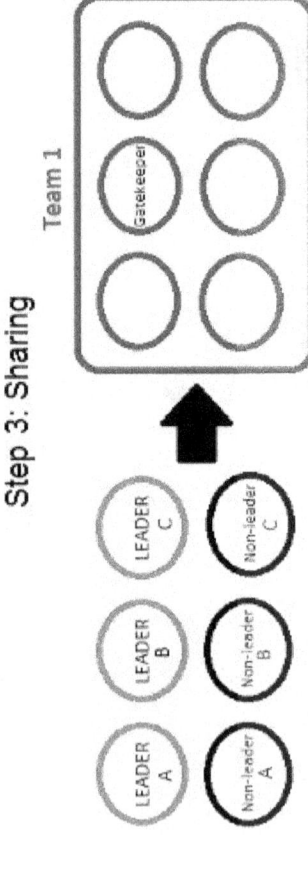

- Leaders and non-leaders come together to share new and old knowledge.
- Everyone will learn and teach everyone. A non-leader can be a leader.
- The dynamics of the team has changed and a gatekeeper is elected to maintain the team and ensure members' personal goals are aligned with team goals. Team goals are aligned with Fun Kite's goals.
- Together, they will achieve goals and develop something better.
- Newly created knowledge is recorded and can be accessed by all Fun Kites members.

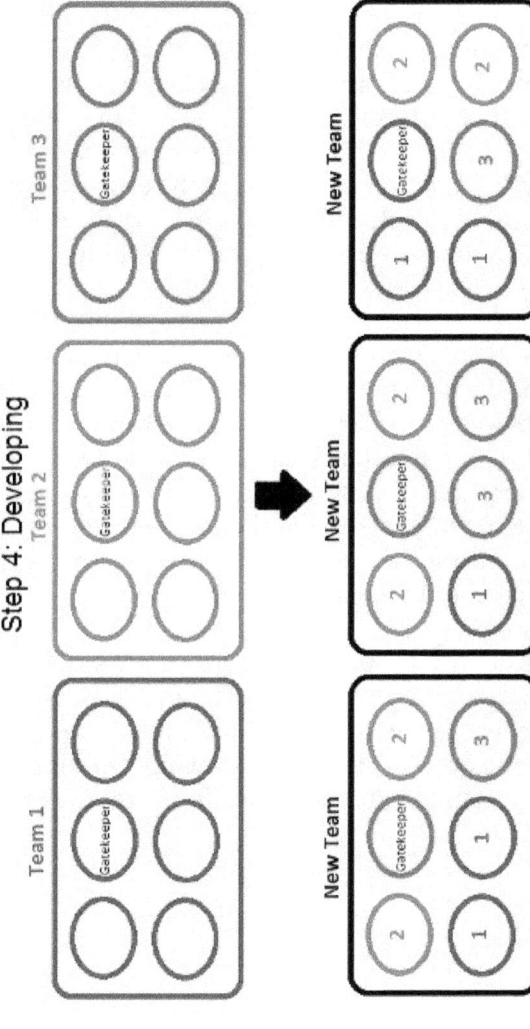

The F Formula encouraged Fun Kites members to be creative and push beyond the boundaries. Some people challenged the norms by experimenting with different types of building materials and designs. Others contributed fresh decorating ideas, developed new flying techniques, and established creative teaching methods. Each project required team members to conduct trial and error and work on actionable tasks. Each team would set small goals, create detailed plans, assign clear roles, learn from failures, make changes, and celebrate small achievements.

Soon, the Fun Kites community became a self-producing pool of innovative ideas. It was not just knowledge. It was shared knowledge. It wasn't a person building a kite, it was about sharing what he or she had built with other people. By sharing knowledge, people were brought together to think about issues differently, improve on existing knowledge, and develop something purposeful that could be shared among the people.

This continuous cycle of gathering and developing knowledge helped Fun Kites to grow and expand. Fun Kites has become an inspiring community where people were continuously learning and growing through the exchange of new and old learning and teaching experiences.

6 GROWING FUN KITES

Several months later, Fun Kites grew bigger and expanded to another park. The two parks were overwhelmed with Fun Kites members. Soon, some of the local public were not happy and had several complaints about the Fun Kites community:

"These people are selfish. They are taking up all the space in the park."

"They are so inconsiderate. They are disturbing the peace and tripping over young children and old people."

Parents of some Fun Kites' members had also expressed certain concerns.

"My son sprained his ankle because he was trying to move around this crowded park."

"The other day an old lady yelled at my daughter for ruining the park."

To make matters worse, a new toy, E-Kite, was launched in the market. It was an electronic kite that had no string attached and was controlled by a remote. It did not require a large and open space to fly, and could even fly as high as a regular kite.

Wendy: "E-Kite is stealing our customers. Parents are pulling their children out of Fun Kites. We have to think of ways to retain them."

Kathy: "Indeed, everyone is saying that E-Kite is the best thing in town. We need to offer something better."

Freddy: "I know parents are considering E-Kite as a safer and better option than Fun Kites. We definitely need to do something."

Father: "People are always complaining. There would always be someone against your ideas. In the midst of all the chaos, you need to stay calm. Do not jump into conclusions. Do not be sidetracked. Divide and focus. There are actually three issues – E-Kite, the complaints by the public, and the complaints by the Fun Kites community."

"You cannot compare E-Kite to Fun Kites because E-Kite is not a kite at all. E-Kite is not really causing your problem. It is just taking advantage of the situation."

"Public opinions matter. But do realize that they do not know the whole story. They do not know Fun Kites as well as you do."

"You should instead focus on the complaints raised by the Fun Kites community. They are not telling you why they are choosing E-Kite. They are telling you why they are not choosing Fun Kites. You have to protect your employees, your Fun Kites members, basically your people and your business."

"Understand that not every complaint requires an action. Ten complaints do not equate to ten solutions. Find the common factor. Enforce one or two solutions and everything else will fall into place."

Freddy analyzed the common factor of the complaints and felt that most of the issues could be resolved if he could find a different venue for the Fun Kites community. The venue had to be large, open, and free of obstacles.

Freddy: "Where do think we could get such a space?"

Wendy: "Perhaps we could rent the sports stadium. However, it might be too expensive."

Kathy: "How about our school field? That is free. I am sure we could work out a schedule with the school to use it on the weekends."

Freddy : "This is a great idea. Let's talk to Mr Art."

Freddy, Wendy, and Kathy met up with Mr Art and brought up the request.

Mr Art: "Children studying at this school can certainly use the school field to fly their kites after school hours. But your community consist of children from other schools as well as adults and parents. I doubt this would be possible."

"Let me tell you a story. Previously, I was teaching a

class of 20 students. Soon, it grew to 25 students and it was hard to manage."

"Then, the class was reduced to 22 and 22 was prefect. I could manage and the students were learning at their best potential. After the school year, the current students left and new ones arrived. People come and people go."

"Even if you are allowed to use the school field, what happens if you have more members? You ought to choose to change something that is not fixed. Changing means having the power to control and shape. Instead of changing the venue, you should change the community."

"Divide the community into smaller groups and allocate them to different parks. Being small would allow flexibility. People could adapt to unforeseen changes quicker. You have to the find the magic number that creates the optimal environment where group members can bond, learn, and grow to their fullest."

"Right now, do not change anything yet. Sometimes, we should place less value on something that is tugging at us with false urgency. Wait and see. Reflect and look far ahead. Take this time to observe the Fun Kites members. Then, find the magic number."

"This issue is telling you something more. Understand that the environment, the venue, the park does not create problems. It is people that create problems. There is a difference between dealing with a problem and resolving a problem. Dealing with a problem is just looking at the surface. Resolving a problem is digging in deeper and fully capturing the true purpose of this problem."

"Once you discover the true purpose, you must act on

it. Give your time, your energy and, your devotion. If you work on it half-hardheartedly, you will not receive genuine returns and will end up being dissatisfied."

Freddy, Wendy, and Kathy reflected on what Mr Art 's advice and had a discussion.

Freddy: "I agree that we should wait and see. Finding the magic number and understanding the issue will take time. We should not implement any drastic changes. For now, we can remind the members on common courtesies (no loud noises, no littering, no intrusion of other people's spaces, etc)."

Kathy: "We should also remind leaders to supervise their team members and to report any incidents to us immediately. After all, kindness is essential to the foundation of Fun Kites."

Weeks went by, and the situation was under control.

Wendy: "Mr Art was right about people coming and people going. During this period, people who did not have faith in Fun Kites or who were not committed to our mission and culture left. Now, we are left with people who truly appreciate Fun Kites and are willingly to help Fun Kites to grow. This will be a good time to experiment and see what the magic number is."

Freddy: "Yes, this is a good time to test the waters. Also, I have been thinking about this issue. I realize that Fun Kites members must learn to coexist with the public. We have to care about the people and the parks."

Kathy: "That is so true. All this time we cared so much about the Fun Kites members, we have neglected to see that we are actually part of the society. Our actions are unknowingly affecting the society."

Freddy: "I feel that there is something missing. We have created a mission and shaped the culture of Fun Kites. We have the F Formula to shape our thinking, learning, and teaching processes. I think we need a set of values to shape us as individuals and to align our personal goals with Fun Kites' goals and mission."

Wendy: "You are right. It is about being good and doing good. Adopting good values helps you to grow internally as a good person. When you do good, it affects other people positively. This strengthens the bonds and commitments towards achieving something far more greater than yourself. Most members of the Fun Kites community have been seeing themselves as a separate entity - one that differs from the society. If we focus on developing individuals' values, we are tying them to the community and the society. They will then appreciate and care for the society. Let's work with the Fun Kites members to develop these values."

And so, they spent the next few months working with the rest of the Fun Kites members to find the magic number and to develop Fun Kites values. Through honest hard work and team work, they finally discovered the magic number and the Fun Kites values.

Fun Kites Values

These values could be applied to oneself (mind, emotions, spirit, body), family, friends, nature, the society, the world, and the universe (Note: The universe refers to everything - the known and unknown. It consists of infinite possibilities.).

Righteous

Be respectful and honest. Be trustworthy and understanding. Pursue justice and have grace. Strive for meaningful impact (instead of benefiting yourself, think of how to genuinely benefit everyone including yourself).

Caring

Be kind, patient, and humble. Value relationships (the good that people do together will exceed the good one does individually). Appreciate life, people, things, events as they are. Treasure present moments. Know when to be contented and when to go forward.

Open-minded

Be courageous and curious. Open up and be vulnerable to embrace all that it is. Be calm and acknowledge all known and unknown (use all senses to observe and be aware). There is no right or wrong perceptions.

Driven

Have strong conviction to push beyond boundaries. Have perseverance and confidence to continuously pursue excellence and purposeful growth. Understand and define clear and realistic needs, commitments, and responsibilities. Achieve goals through genuine passion and honest hard work. Be accountable (be responsible and answerable for your actions).

Balanced

Know when to move, when to stop, and when to change. Understand limitations (weaknesses, time, resources, unknown factors), the cycle of nature (what goes up must come down), and your life (where you truly belong and your purpose). Seek synchronization (not peak performance but a performance that balances with other performances to achieve ultimate potential).

All Fun Kites would develop these values through the following ways:
- Learning kite building, decorating, flying, and teaching skills
- Using the F Formula
- Working on projects as a team

Apart from sharing the Fun Kites mission and culture, all leaders were required to enforce Fun Kites values. Freddy also launched a "My Values" campaign. After every Fun Kites gathering, the children would write down a value that they had learned or used or taught on a kite-shape sticker. They would stick the stickers on their chests and proudly share their experiences with their parents and other Fun Kites members. This not only reinforced Fun Kites values among the members but also translated the values to their parents.

Fun Kites members were also encouraged to adopt these values at school and share them with their friends and classmates. These values allowed genuine connections to flourish within the community as well as with the society. Thus, creating happier and more fulfilling personal lives.

Many parents began to see the positive progression in their children. They were glad that their children were part of the Fun Kites community.

However, most parents would pull their children out of the community after six to eight months. Freddy understood that community, the society, and the people were constantly changing. After all, moving on would enable the children to use what they had learned to establish something meaningful for themselves in the future.

Freddy knew he had to adapt and hence continuously promoted Fun Kites so as to ensure a steady flow of new members. It was not really about maintaining profits as profits came naturally. It was about maintaining the cycle of human connections, the flow of ideas, and the continuous path of teaching, learning, and growing the right values and skills. That was what really mattered.

7 GOING BEYOND FUN KITES

One day, Freddy visited Mr Art.

Mr Art: "Last Friday, I was with my nephew at one of your Fun Kites gatherings. Jimmy is 8 years old and has attention deficit disorder."

"When he was playing with the other children, I was amazed to see that he had so much faith and trust in himself. This was because the other children did not judge him. Instead, they opened up and believed in Jimmy."

"Children, unlike adults, are filled with innocence. Their emotions and expressions are real and non-judgmental. They express themselves genuinely so as to let others know how they truly feel because they know a person's feelings are important."

"In their world, ideal and reality are intertwined. They see infinite possibilities. In their minds, every single day is an opportunity to play, learn, and grow. It is within themselves that they found the courage and the determination to fearlessly seek to venture the unknown."

"Unfortunately, in the adult world, it is different. Adults have responsibilities. And with responsibilities come doubts, assumptions, and the constant need to control. They have forgotten how to let go, be spontaneous, and play."

"They have honest intentions but because of fear they lost their courage and moved way from their true selves. They forgot how to be genuine and how to fight for what they believe in."

"Sadly, they fail to live in the present moment. Hence, they fail to appreciate the joys of what the world can offer and missed out on beautiful life connections. Sometimes, people need to stop, reflect, and appreciate NOW."

"Fun Kites has created an environment for parents to connect with their children. They are given the opportunity to learn how to play again. The beauty lies in learning from their children. It must be an extraordinary moment for parents to stand in their children's shoes to feel how they felt and to see what they saw. One ought to be thankful for such special moments that no money or great invention can create. This is truly unique to each individual who is willingly to open up and be free."

"When these children grow up, they would retain some Fun Kites values. I am sure they have inspired their families, friends, and the society. Freddy, when you grow up, reconnect with them in the future. You will be amazed how Fun Kites has impacted their lives and how they have impacted the society."

And so, Freddy set up a website to maintain contacts with the old and new Fun Kites members. With the help of Wendy, he continued to improve and expand Fun Kites.

Many years later, Freddy reconnected with many old Fun Kites members. He developed great relationships with them. Some even contributed back to Fun Kites.

Kathy and Richie became school teachers. They frequently shared the F Formula and imparted Fun Kites values to their students.

Beth (one of the girls decorating under the tree) became a famous artist. Together with Fun Kites, she launched the yearly "Fun Kite Painting" competition.

Sam became a charity advocate. He supplied kite building materials to the less fortunate children and encouraged them to join Fun Kites.

Rachel became a musician. She worked with the Fun Kites to developed the Fun Kites Synchronized Flying program where children would fly kites together in musical harmony.

Phil became a psychologist. He assisted in improving the Fun Kites Leadership program and volunteered to train new leaders.

Freddy began to see what really mattered was the flow of values through shared knowledge or a product (in this case it would be learning of kite building, decorating, flying and teaching skills).

Flow of Fun Kites Values

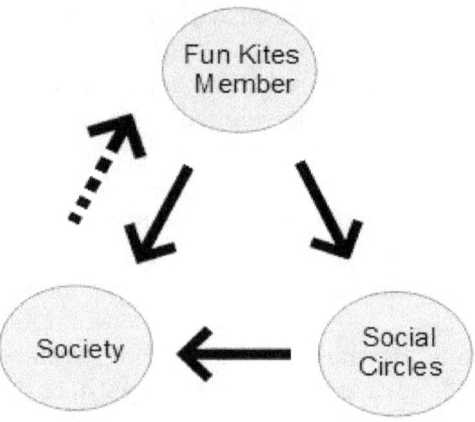

A Fun Kites member's behaviors and words could be seen as a reflection of Fun Kites values. Hence, every interaction would be an opportunity for a transfer of Fun Kites values.

Fun Kites values would flow from a Fun Kites member to his/her social circles (family, friends, etc) as well as to the society (people outside of the social circles – schoolmates, people at the park, etc). Members of his/her social circles would also assist in transferring the values to the society.

As the Fun Kite member integrated with the society, these values would change. By reaching out and reestablishing the relationship, these Fun Kites values would be revived. He or she could then bring significant contributions back to the Fun Kites community.

Good values are crucial to the development of a person, a business, and a society. How a person contribute back to his/her family, the workplace, businesses (as a customer), and the society would depend on the kind of values that he/she has learned from his/her family, the workplace, businesses and the society.

***

Freddy understood the power of shared knowledge and its meaningful impact on people's lives. So, he started writing this book. When Freddy finished writing, he was not sure if this might or might not help someone. All he knew was that if he did not publish it, the odds of changing someone's life was an absolute zero. Hence, he took a leap of faith and published it.

By sharing his inspirational journey, Freddy hoped that this book has changed your thinking and your actions as well as helped you to fulfill your purpose, push beyond boundaries, and inspire others.

ACKNOWLEDGMENTS

I want to thank the following as this book would never be possible without these brilliant minds and thoughts.

Fear and Trembling by Soren Kierkegaard

Harvard Business Review – harvardbusiness.org/harvardbusiness/ideacast

Knowledge @ Wharton – knowledge.wharton.upenn.edu

The Energy Bus by Jon Gordon

The Meditations By Marcus Aurelius

The Mozi translated by Ian Johnston

The Noticer by Andy Andrew

The ONE Thing by Gary Keller and Jay Papasan

The Way of Life by Lao Tzu

Your Inner Will by Piero Ferrucci

**The Kite Story
Freddy and his Kite**
A story about entrepreneurship, creativity, and life

Unique Edu Ltd.

Bring Education to the Next Level

www.ingramcontent.com/pod-product-compliance
Lightning Source LLC
Chambersburg PA
CBHW061444180526
45170CB00004B/1549